Gabriel Jackson

EDINBURGH MASS

CONTENTS

Commissioned by The Very Revd Graham Forbes, Provost of St Mary's Episcopal Cathedral, Edinburgh, with additional funds provided by the Leche Trust and the Kenneth Leighton Trust.

First performed by the choir of St Mary's Episcopal Cathedral, directed by Matthew Owens, on St Cecilia's Day 2001. *Edinburgh Mass* is recorded by St Mary's Cathedral choir, directed by Matthew Owens, on Delphian DCD34027.

Duration: 13 minutes

MUSIC DEPARTMENT

OXFORD
UNIVERSITY PRESS

Edinburgh Mass

GABRIEL JACKSON

KYRIE

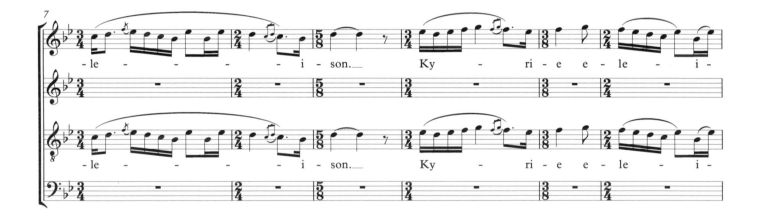

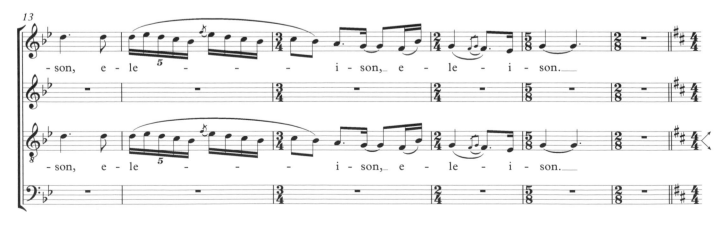

Printed in Great Britain

OXFORD UNIVERSITY PRESS, MUSIC DEPARTMENT, GREAT CLARENDON STREET, OXFORD OX2 6DP

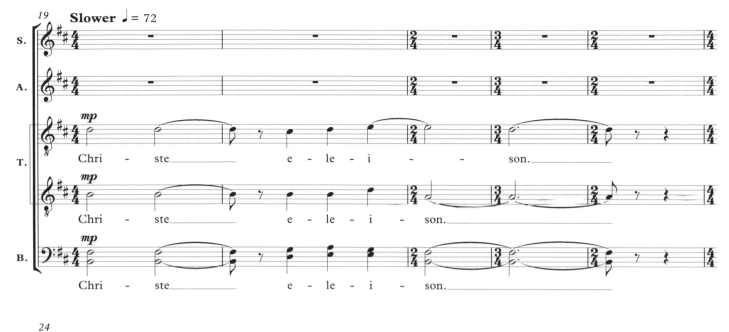

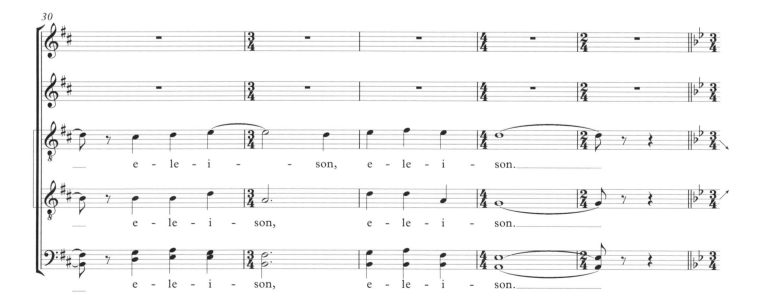

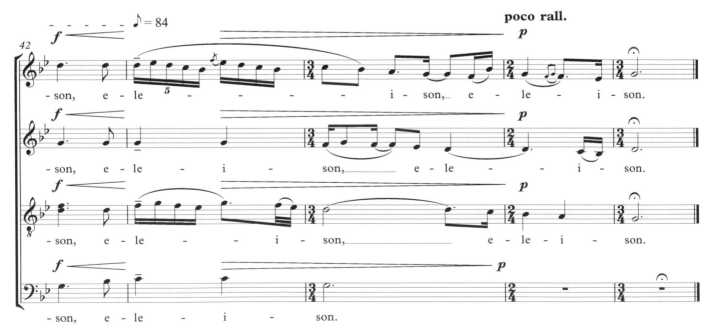

GLORIA

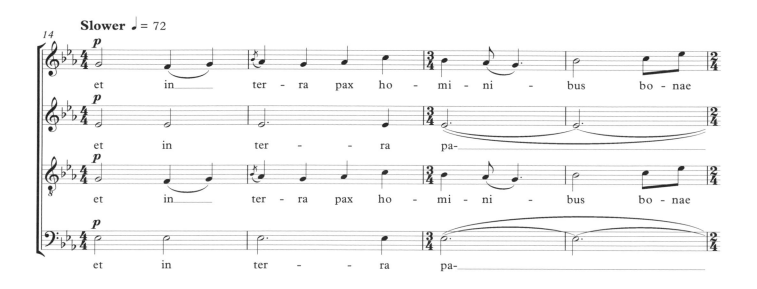

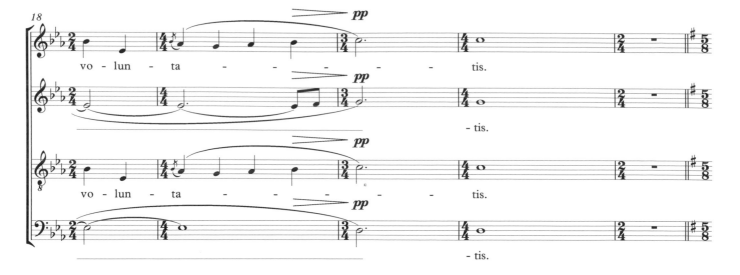

*give each note a slight 'ping' (not as strong as an accent)

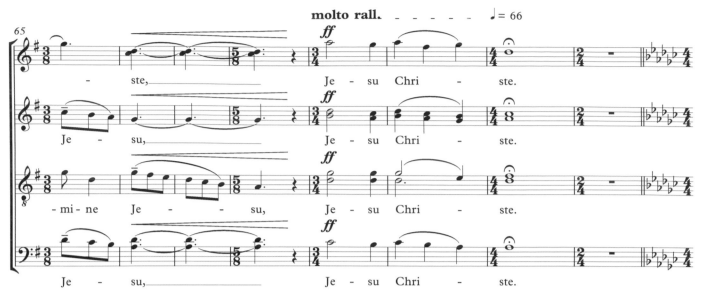

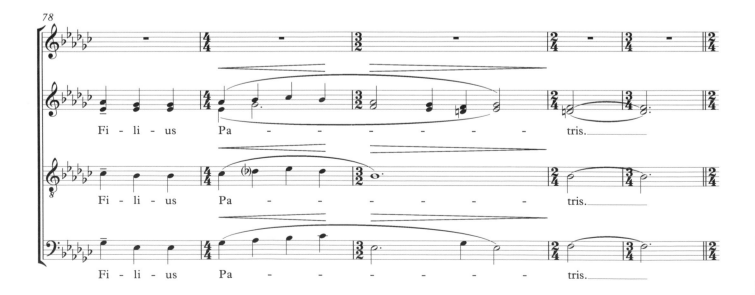

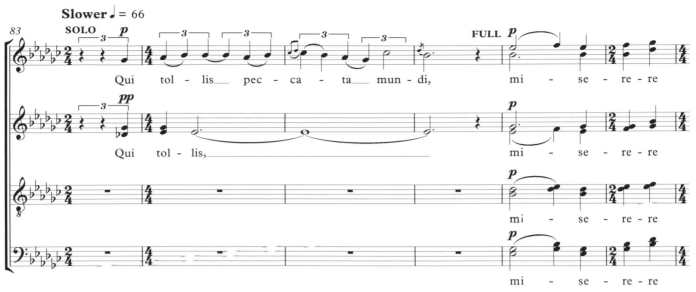

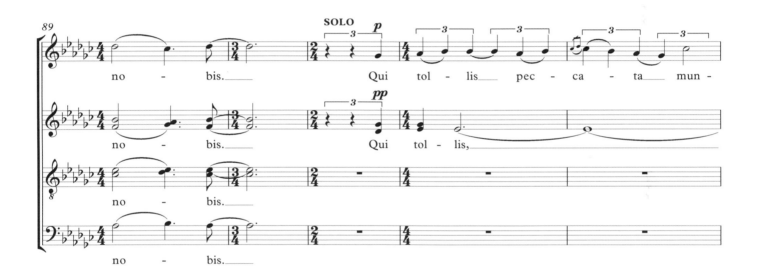

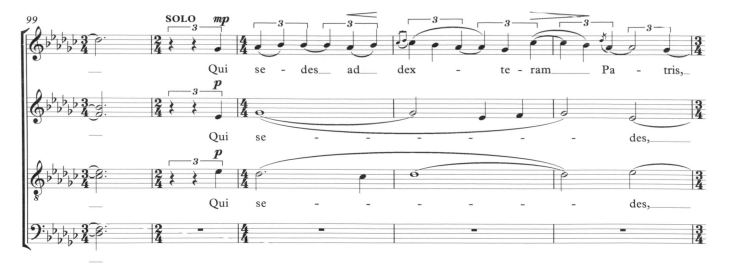

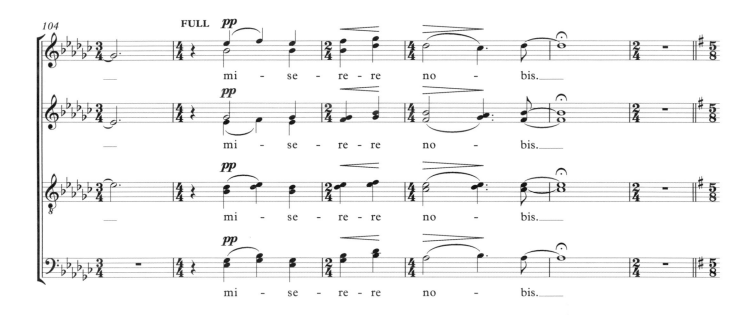

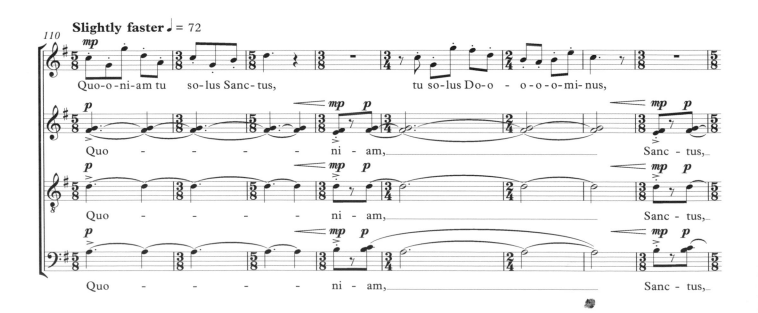

SANCTUS & BENEDICTUS

*accented notes *poco sforzando*

Light, dancing ♩ = 112

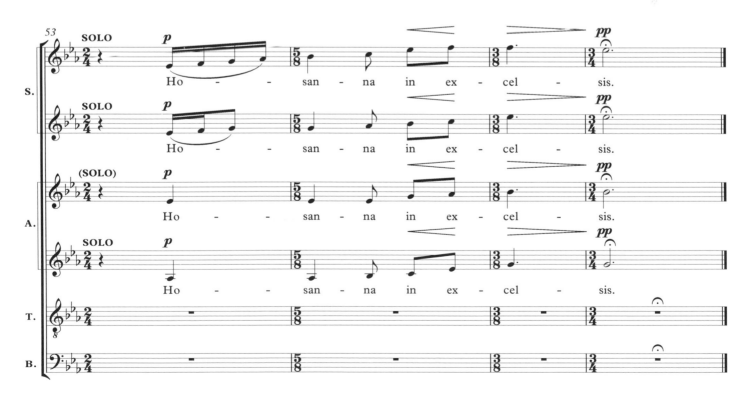

AGNUS DEI

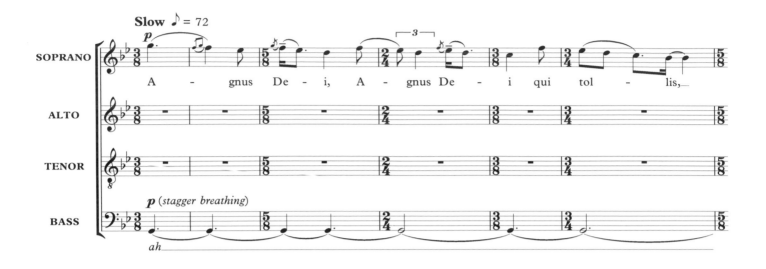

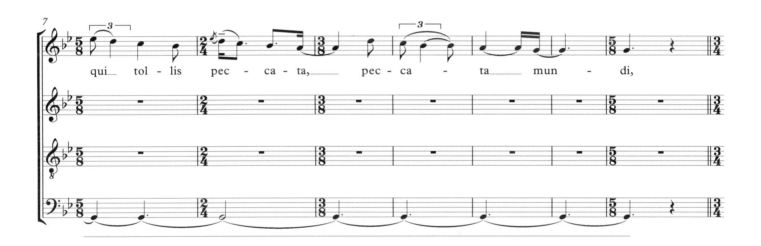

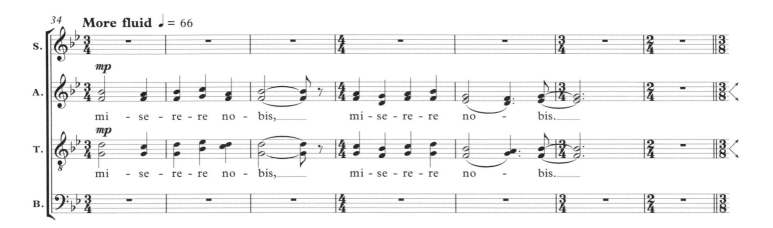

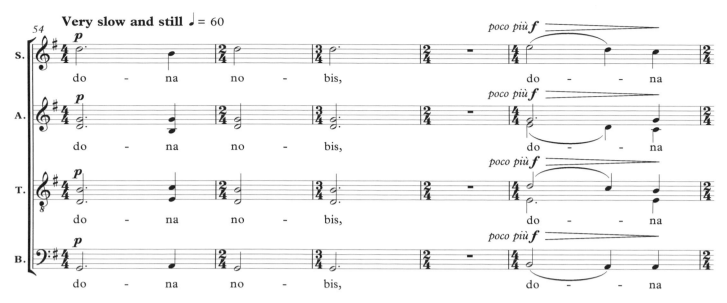

Processed in England by Enigma Music Production Services, Amersham, Bucks.
Printed in England by Halstan & Co. Ltd., Amersham, Bucks.

Brockley, January–April 2001